I0536293

Accidents Will Happen

Accidents Will Happen

essays & photos

Ryan Rickrode

matinee
press

ISBN: 978-1-970920-00-0

Published by Matinee Press
www.matineepress.com

Copyedited by Courtney Allen

Cover Photography
& Design by Ryan Rickrode

"Six Feet from the Sun" previously appeared
in *The Common* in 2013 and *The Good Men
Project* in in 2014.

"Consuming Fire" previously appeared in
Bright Bones: Contemporary Montana Writing in
2018.

"Accidents Will Happen" previously
appeared in *The Windhover* in 2024.

To all the official and honorary
Rickrodes, Olivers, Ecksteins,
Owenses, and Richs

Contents

My Father's Philosophy of Bees

They have kings. They have armies. They go to war.
—*The Book of Beasts*, translated by T.H. White

Bees. Damn bees. Or wasps. (Whatever.) I don't care what they're called. When roofers blunder into the gutters, eaves, and gables where wasps have their nests—

well, I personally retreat. Climb halfway down the ladder and jump the hell off. Strip off a length of old siding and there they are and they are already flying. They scramble like fighter jets, and I too am scrambling, because when I'm stung I swell. My hand will be fat for a week.

My father's approach is otherwise.

Dad is (or seems to be) impervious to bees. He works hard and hurts when he comes home—sore back, sore knees, cramps (his calves clench like teeth)—but as far as I can tell, no bee can wound him. Instead of reaching into the trailer for a can of bee spray (which has range of thirty feet), he climbs the ladder with a pry bar and knocks down the nest.

This, to me, seems counterproductive, more head-on and less tactical than I (who must also stand in the cloud of bees he's created) would prefer. He once knocked a wasps' nest from the dogwood tree in our backyard and then sucked it up with the lawn tractor. Problem solved. (Although how did he empty the mower bags after? I don't know.)

Or once when I was a kid, he gave me a drill and told me to put a new hole in the old pole so we could re-string our clothesline. I put the bit to the metal, squeezed the trigger, and out of the top of the pole came a wasp. *Huh.* I began again: another wasp. It occurred to me then that my father had asked me to drill a hole straight through the core of the wasp mothership. I returned to the workshop.

"This is stupid. I'm not doing it."

Dad made a counterproposal: "I'll drill the hole. You take this can of bee spray and shoot them as they fly out." (As if the spray would kill them instantly? As if my aim were that good? What were we thinking?)

Dad began to drill. A bee flew out, landed on the back of my trigger hand, and stabbed me (swollen for a week). I dropped the can and fled, like a sensible person. *To hell with this.*

My father stayed behind, drilled the hole, and the clothesline stands in my parents' backyard to this day.

Six Feet from the Sun

When you're a carpenter's son there are things you don't tell your mother. The old asbestos siding Dad had you driving nails into, for instance. Or the ceiling fan he wired without first shutting off the power. How you close your eyes when you bring the chop saw's round whirling blade down on a length of spouting so you won't get any flecks of metal in your eyes. How it just seems safer that way.

We were on a roof in a thunderstorm once, two stories up. The rain had caught us off guard, with large patches of sheeting still exposed when it started coming down. To have taken shelter then would have meant abandoning the house to serious water damage. Dad kept saying, "I'm gonna end up buying the ceiling." He was so steeped in tunnel vision I'm not sure he registered the lightning.

What I remember is the acoustics, the peculiar way the thunder seemed to roll across the roofs around us. When he sent me down for ice and water shield to seal up the bare patches I made the cuts quickly, with my back turned. I didn't want to risk seeing my father get struck by lightning.

When we roof, we start early, pushing back noon as far as we can because that's when the roofs get hot. We start when the summer air is still cool enough to raise the hair on my arms. The sun is hidden behind the mountains, and the neighborhood looks empty. We spread the tarps, prop the ladders, pull on our roof boots. If we tore off the old shingles yesterday, we'll uncoil the extension cords and hook up the air lines for the nail guns. I lean into the trailer to switch on the compressor then pull my head out fast—it kicks on loud, a rapid thump that eclipses the calm of the morning.

By ten-thirty the sun is firmly in the sky. The surface of the roof is radiating a heat of its own. If you lay the bare skin of your arm or your leg against the shingles—or the tar paper or even just the wood sheeting—you'll be burned. We once laid a wall thermometer on the sun-warmed shingles of a shed roof, just to see, and the needle maxed out at a hundred and twenty degrees. "It must be broken," I said, but Dad disagreed, and now I'm not sure. He likes to joke with homeowners that it's hotter for us on the roof because we're closer to the sun. He says, "We were six feet from the sun. I threw my tape measure up there and checked. Don't try this at home."

So we don't hesitate. We go at it with pry bars and shovels. We

view from the roof

jobsite

wrench up shingles and nails and felt. We work until the roof is stripped to the sheeting, then we cover it again, with ice and water shield and aluminum drip edge and long sheets of plastic "felt" to protect it from the constant threat of summer storms. By now it's two o'clock and our day is ending. Or it's only eleven-thirty, and Dad will decide the other side of the roof is going to get torn off too, and we'll continue until two or three or four, until the tools are too hot to hold and the tarry strips of ice and water shield start scuffing and smearing beneath our boots like we're walking on molasses.

We'll return the next day to tack down the shingles. We work our way from the bottom to the top, me laying them down and him shooting nails or vice versa. We stairstep our way up the roof, and when we reach the peak we own it in a way the homeowners never will. We know it in a way they can't—the texture of the shingles, the pull of gravity at that pitch, the tiny flaws they'll never see.

I grew up in a house built by my great-grandfather and learned how to use a drill press before I learned to read. I am—or could be—a fourth-generation carpenter. There's a picture of me as a child up to my belly in deck joists, plastic hammer in hand, and another of me, even younger, standing up to my thighs in my dad's work boots. I have no memory of being taught to use the band saw, only my father standing behind me, his hands on

photo of the author as a child,
hanging next to hammers in the workshop

above: the author's father, grandfather, and great-grandfather building an addition to his grandfather's house

below: bundles of shingles on the roof of that same house

mine, reminding me how it's done. At his father's viewing, my father pointed out to me the furniture stain on my grandfather's hands. He was buried with it in the swirls of his fingers.

In the summer and the winter, I'm a roofer, a carpenter, a cabinetmaker, but in the fall and spring, I'm a grad student and a teacher. An academic. Being away from the work used to trouble me. As an undergrad, I would call my dad every morning on my way to class, and I could gauge the time of day by the tone in his voice. When I moved to Montana, two time zones away, to pursue my master's degree in creative writing, my calls always seemed to catch him when the sun was getting hot and he had no time to talk.

Without pointing or nodding or even glancing, at work Dad will sometimes say things like "Put it on that side" or "Put it over there." When he says the tool you're looking for is "in the back of the truck," he could mean that the tool is on— or under—the backseat of the truck, that the tool is somewhere in the bed of the truck, or even that the tool is in the trailer attached to the truck. His vagueness drives me crazy, but then I catch myself saying, "I need that over there."

Your brain works differently in the sun. Your cognitive functions melt down into simple cause-and-effect reasoning. You think in images instead of words, and you don't waste time saying things that don't need to be said.

shenanigans

taking some measurements

"Give me the pliers," I once told my dad while a friend watched us work.

"Shouldn't you say 'please'?" she asked.

"There's no time for 'please' when you're working," I said, and Dad nodded as he passed me the tool.

It's no coincidence that the tools we use tend to be named either for what they look like or for what they do (or, in the case of the pipe clamp, both). On the one hand you've got *claw* hammers, *needle-nosed* pliers, and the "Turbo Pancake" air compressor in the trailer. On the other you've got the pry bar, the digging bar, and the wrecking bar, which are all the same thing. The name changes depending on how you use it, like the conjugations of a verb. The names are short and staccato, words your tongue can grab hold of even as the sun pares down your vocabulary.

I've always wanted to be a writer, except when I was very young I wanted to read utility meters. I wanted to wear the boots, the hat, and the Maglite. I was in preschool, and Dad was working for the borough in the mornings, reading utility meters and delivering late notices to provide us with health insurance while my mother stayed home with me and my siblings. After work, he'd come home and head to the garage, where he built furniture with his father. They were working on getting a business up and running. When I told my father I wanted to read

a roll-off box gets delivered,
soon to be filled with dead shingles

bundles of shingles on a roof in the winter

meters, he ruffled my hair and said, "No you don't."

I've always wanted to be like my father, to embody his work ethic, his humor, his grace. I feel good when I answer the phone and people mistake me for him. I was once told we eat the same, both of us hunched over our plates, and I took it as a compliment. I've also been told we look the same, and that's true: we've got the same nose, the same cowlicks, the same smile. We both look like his father and—I'm certain—like his grandfather. I don't know what he looked like, but I'm sure I could pick him from a lineup.

The sound of my father heaving a bundle of shingles up onto his shoulders is a growl you might mistake for anger. It amazes me the things he lifts on his own—whole lengths of kitchen cabinets, the dump trailer's thick metal tailgate, the box trailer itself when the ball hasn't quite lined up with the hitch. He's past fifty, but he can still lift more than me, and he runs rings around the guys who still gather once a year for basketball reunions. At the jobsite he snatches bundles of shingles out of my arms when he sees me trying to lug them up the ladder. It's been almost nine years since my grandfather died, and Dad has gotten used to working alone.

But when two or three people are working together the sound of the machinery can be almost like music. Not because it's pleasant (though the air nailers do make a satisfying snap), but because every

Dad checks on a roof job
on his way home from a funeral

going up: Dad on a scissor lift

sound is purposeful and distinct. When we lift things together, Dad always says, "On three. *Three!*" and we lift. There is no "One, two." We move things like it's an Olympic sport, gracefully lifting and rotating couches and tables without speaking, maneuvering through narrow doorways and into new rooms, never banging a finished side against the walls, not once.

He reads my stuff—the fiction, the nonfiction, all of it. He likes when our shared experiences show up in the stories: that floor we refinished in Hamilton Heights, that know-it-all customer who wouldn't let us be. "You can't make that shit up," he says, a phrase he's picked up from one of my fiction professors.

Sometimes he'll ask what I've been up to, and I'll say, "Just finished a book," and he'll say, "Reading or writing?" as if neither would surprise him, as if writing a book is something I could do on a rainy afternoon, and I love that I have a father who believes in me that much. I often wish writing were more like carpentry so I could better share it with him. He asks me questions about the process—how do I know what direction to take a story? Where do I get my ideas? When did I know this character would do that? He talks about my stories as if they're solid things that have been assembled and sanded, but for me, writing them often feels more like roaming through the dark, armed only with the Maglite of hope and intuition.

framing a shed

looking down through a skylight

Here's a story: Once in the workshop, while he was lying flat on his back draining the dirty water that had condensed inside the big air compressor tank, Dad told me about my great-grandfather, Paul Rickrode. He was an engineer who travelled around the world repairing massive industrial hammers. In this story Paul was at a factory in England. Picture him in a white button-down shirt and a hard hat, an official representative of the Chambersburg Engineering Co.—the company where my grandfather would work for years as a shop superintendent, where my dad would work as a draftsman until the place shut down in the 90s. Paul was inspecting a broken impactor and quickly identified the cause of the problem, a broken piston rod or rocker arm or maybe a hydraulic leak—Dad doesn't remember. What he knows is that Paul had two options: have the impactor dismantled, the part replaced, and the machine put back together—a painstaking and expensive process that would hold up production for days—or he could slide under the machine and repair it himself. When Paul emerged from underneath the impactor, his clean white shirt was streaked with grease.

My dad paused here and sat up so we could exchange drip pans, a full one for an empty one, and then, before lying back down, said, "I'd like to think I'd do the same."

Consuming
Fire

The night of the fire I missed two calls from my friend Holly, who had family on the mountain that was burning.

No one could get ahold of her uncle, and for an hour or so it was looking like Holly would have to drive up and find him—he was probably running heavy machinery, deaf to phone calls and flames alike—but by the time I called her back, Scot had been accounted for. The only thing left for us to do was to brainstorm activities for the evening.

"We could drive out and look at the fire," Holly said, "but there's not much to see."

The next morning a professor of mine who lived on the mountain said there were "three-hundred-year-old trees shooting flames thirty feet into the air."

He said the fire shone like city lights in the pines.

~

I'm surprised when I walk out of the video store and it's raining ash.

So complete is the apparent lack of concern among the Montanans, you'd never guess that just five miles outside of town two thousand acres of land are burning.

I'm an Easterner for sure: I long for the yellow grass on the mountains to turn Appalachian green in the spring and am still surprised when I wake in the morning and the air smells like campfire smoke. Missoula, Montana sits in a valley that once was the bottom of a glacial lake. Sometimes, as I walk along the river, I imagine myself walking underwater, stirring up sediment, but then I look up at the mountains and the sky, and I can't imagine enough water to turn those ridges into shorelines.

My eyes won't adjust to the mountains. They are the same shape as the Pennsylvania hills I grew up in but much larger. They throw off my depth perception—always bigger and farther off than I would guess.

Two thousand acres of land: That's three square miles of fire and you'd never know it, not by the looks on their faces. This lack of concern, it's strange to me because fire so often draws our eyes. We arrange furniture around our TVs the way our ancestors once arranged themselves around campfires and hearths.

Even the smallest flame: that milky flicker of the candle in my hands at church on Christmas Eve always arrests my gaze, a light come into the darkness, God like a flame—in, but not of, this world.

My advisor, who's lived in Montana all her life, tells me the reason: Montanans know the difference between close and too close.

~

After class, I asked Holly to drive me out to the fire—I wanted to see it for myself, wanted to grasp the magnitude of it—and she agreed, on the condition that we drive through without stopping. She wasn't going to be one of those "gawkers."

Out the car window I saw pines glittering orange, whole mountains shrouded in smoke, and more of both around each bend.

The road kept winding, the smoke grew thicker.

Along the side of the road were signs that said "NO STOPPING," but every pull-off we passed was crowded with people—*gawkers*—watching the Forest Service helicopters swooping buckets into the river and then flying up the mountain to drop their loads.

At one point the road we were driving ran along a ridge that sits above the water, and we saw a helicopter—gigantic up close—dive past the car and below the surface of the road.

Down in the river, where the helicopters were filling their buckets, people floated through the smoke on fat black inner tubes, and I thought of a schoolyard legend Holly once told me about scuba diver bones in the woods surrounding Whitefish Lake.

Weeks later I will learn that the Clark Fork was closed to floaters the very next day, and when I recount the story about the floaters to my freshmen writing students, one of them will raise his hand and grin. "That was me."

~

"The human body," writes the poet Kazim Ali, "is a bundle of sticks in a chemical process similar to combustion," and so much hinges on those words *similar to*. They are the distance between the hand of a child and the burner on a stove, the space between the earth and the sun.

The stars, each one a fire that could consume our whole planet, are beautiful because they're far off.

~

The night of the fire my professor wandered down his road past the truck stop, where deer and sheep driven from the mountain were milling about.

He stopped at a church parking lot, where a group of people had assembled with lawn chairs and beer. They were watching a house on the ridge, waiting to see if it would burn, and my professor—whose own home was dangerously close to those flames—watched them watch the flames.

"Nobody was rooting for the fire," he said, "but nobody was rooting against it either."

~

The Tuesday morning *Missoulian* reports that the fire "raced across

150 acres and crested the ridge-line while residents—some less than 100 yards below the fire's down-slope edge—scrambled to water sun-baked yards and removed personal belongings."

Among the first to spot the smoke was a seven-year-old girl playing on her porch. "I heard a 'poof' like a firework," she told a reporter. "Then I saw smoke."

There's a surprising honesty in the strong verbs and dramatic modi-fiers of those early newspaper ar-ticles: "Fighting Back," "Circling The Blaze," "Shifting Flames." The reporters aren't pretending they don't find the fire exciting, not even after a full week of coverage: "As the day warmed, the 3,400-acre wildfire moved northwest *belching out giant plumes of smoke* that could be seen throughout the Missoula Valley."

The fire occupies the front page of the paper for a week before it is displaced, and as the fire cools so does the prose: "The fire was 35 percent contained at nightfall." Another week and the fire is buried deep within the paper: "West Riverside Blaze Winding Down," "Crews Starting Mop-Up Phase."

~

A year later I visit a friend, a Montanan, who is stationed as a lookout for the Forest Service. I count eighty steps from the top of the mountain to the top of his watchtower. Beyond us, below, the tops of pines are whipping in the breeze.

Was all this once underwater?

Once an hour he takes up his binoculars and scans the horizon for smoke, of which there's plenty, but none worth radioing in. It's drifting over from fires far off in Idaho.

He sets the binoculars aside. If you look too much, he says, it'll drive you crazy.

But there are perks. He talks about the stars as if they're an event. He mentions them casually, speculates about what the smoke will do to their visibility, half jokes that he would like to buy a tower of his own one day.

His favorite time is sunset, but today there is no sun. The sun is an orange smudge that doesn't set so much as it burns out and disappears. No stars either, so we look northwest to Helena and watch the city lights flicker like candles through the haze.

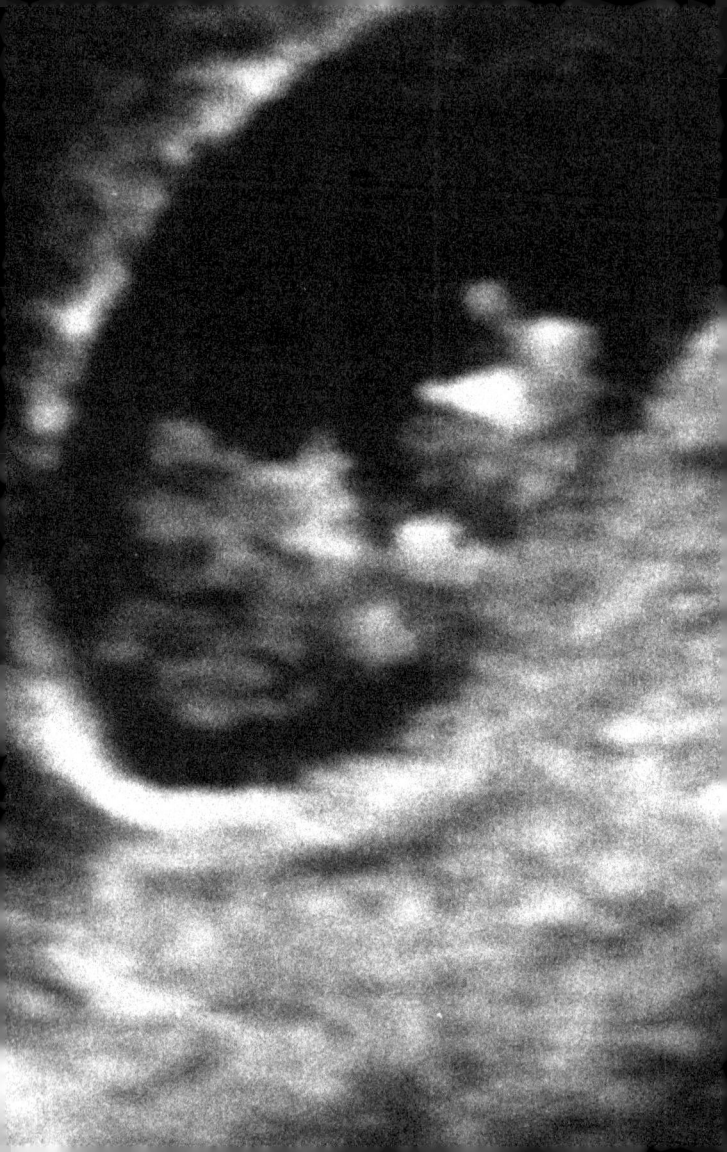

Accidents
Will Happen

"Now my dears," said old Mrs. Rabbit one morning, "You may go into the fields or down the lane, but don't go into Mr. McGregor's garden. Your Father had an accident there."

—*The Tale of Peter Rabbit* by Beatrix Potter

Three weeks ago, while we were reading in bed, my wife took my hand and I felt our baby move. I don't know how to describe it. "Flutter" is the word Anna uses most often, or she'll say, "The baby is being flippy. I wish you could feel it." This time I felt it. It was like making contact with a spirit— the candles flicker, the table lifts up, and even the medium looks startled—or so I imagine, except this was happy. I want to say it was the happiest moment of my life so far, it really might be, but it's so unlike anything else I've experienced—*sui generis* in the fullest sense of the phrase—that I don't know how to measure it against other moments. Is it greater or less than kneeling in Anna's driveway on Christmas Eve with a ring? Or how does it compare with the priest wrapping his stole around her hands and mine to signify and seal the vows we'd just made? Or my baptism at eighteen, that moment when I was lifted out of a quick cold creek, from death into life? Rightly or wrongly the word *sacrament* comes to mind, Saint Augustine's definition: a visible form of an invisible grace. As if something could be weighty and weightless all at once.

How do you measure this? What compares?

My father says he's never felt anything as soft as a just-born baby. After our second ultrasound, five months into the pregnancy, I texted him: "The baby's femur is one-and-three-quarter inches long." He sent back a picture of his fingertip next to a tape measure: two crooked knuckles, an inch and three quarters. His carpenter's hands are about the roughest you'll ever see, big fingers that are speckled with paint, or with tar, or they're scabbed with cement.

The other day he came to campus to see my new office. It was the quickest of tours. "That was my dad," I said to the student who came in just after. "He was up this way for a doctor's appointment."

The student said, "I hope his hand gets better soon."

"No, no," I said, "he was here for an appointment with his heart doctor. That's how his hands always look." I'd barely registered the giant wad of gauze wrapped around his fingers, and Dad hadn't thought to mention it. That's how it's always been. A favorite show in our house growing up was *Home Improvement*, which, as far as we were concerned, was a show about our dad. In the show Tim Allen plays Tim "The Tool Man" Taylor, the accident-prone host of *Tool Time* (a fictional show within the show) who always takes things too far. His over-powered floor sander sands a hole through the floor. His charcoal grill takes

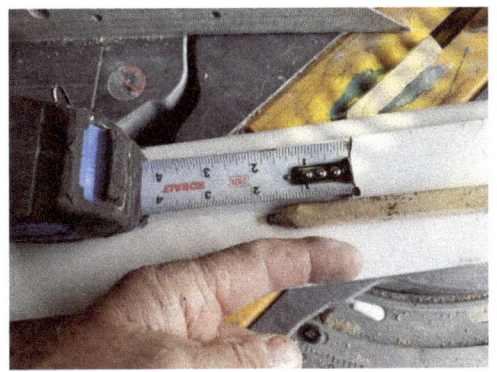

an inch and three quarters

off like a rocket. He falls through a roof. He shocks himself often, on light sockets, power outlets, and dishwashers. He bends over to pick up a dropped object and (my favorite) accidentally superglues his forehead to a table.

The American Academy of Pediatrics says the mattress in our cradle is too small. There is a dangerous gap. Perhaps we should spend three hundred dollars on a bassinet.

What makes it dangerous? I ask. The cradle is the one I slept in as a baby, it was built by my father.

My wife begins to scroll.

Like many (most? all?) first-time American parents, I am learning that everything is dangerous—even items specifically for babies. Little blankets, stuffed bunnies, they come with ominous tags reminding us how easy it is for an infant to suffocate.

Sometimes this seems ridiculous, sometimes it doesn't. As I write it's 2023 and I've grown—what's the right word? accustomed? weary? resigned? inured?—to the riskiness of just about everything. Three years ago, in the first days of the pandemic, my wife and I went to the grocery store together, wondering if the trip would cause us to die. We Lysol-ed everything we brought in. We stockpiled jugs of water in the basement because we'd heard "the infrastructure might fail." Three days before Christmas an outdoor conversation with a COVID-stricken friend left me wondering if I should skip the holiday or risk killing (this is what it felt like at the time) my whole family.

My family is fine, as is my friend, and COVID seems less scary now, but my wife and I still sometimes fear the grocery store and the movies and our places of work—you always hear about another mass shooting. We take a deep breath, tell ourselves a true-enough story about probability and statistics, and then we go on.

On the drive home from our first ultrasound, looking through the black-and-white swirls, I said to Anna, "Are we having a baby or a tropical storm?"

This was about eight weeks in, when we could hardly believe the pregnancy was real. Anna's symptoms so far had been mild, and she wasn't yet showing. Doubting, we'd done a second test: two blue lines, but we still felt unsure.

Here now was proof, pictures of a tadpole-ish creature, all legs and a head (and the contours of a face!). When we got home I framed the shots and kept them close. For a day or two I even carried them around. They felt more real to me than the baby itself, hidden in Anna's womb, and it dawned on me why the Old Testament is so forceful in its condemnation of images and idols: even an accurate image can pull us away from what's real.

When my wife's grandfather was nearing the end of his life, her uncle would go to him, saying, "Can I borrow your chainsaw? Can I borrow your ladder?" Granddaddy, always generous, would say yes, and

Dale would take the tools away. Granddaddy, I think, knew what was up, but the game was important, and in the end he won: "We found two other chainsaws when we cleaned out his shed."

My dad is a good thirty years younger than my wife's grandfather would be today, and it was just two or three years ago that I watched him ascend a ladder with a chainsaw while I held a rope he'd lashed to a dead limb, torso-sized where it branched from the trunk. My job: pull hard as the branch falls, don't let it land on the house. (We were mostly successful—the house was grazed but not damaged, and the only limb lost was from the tree.)

I thought of this episode when my sister, who works at a building supply store, called me on the phone, excited that she'd come up with a Christmas present for Dad that the whole family could go in on, a tool he didn't have: the Milwaukee M18 Pole Saw (read: chainsaw on a stick). I said, Perfect.

It'll make things easier on his knees, which are all out of cartilage, but it won't keep him off ladders—I have no illusions about that, and I'm not really bothered by it. I've known all my life that there's a small but real chance my dad could end up in Carpenter Valhalla. I've written elsewhere, once in fiction and once in an essay, about watching him patch a roof in a rainstorm with lightning flashing in the background and me below, cutting pieces and ferrying them up the ladder.

He's fallen off ladders—not off the top, thank goodness, and usually into bushes—and I once almost watched him dance backwards off the edge of a roof. (It was, on the radio, a Mix 95.1 "Party Weekend" and "Everybody Dance Now" had just come blaring through.) Just the other week he was over at my house removing a shattered bulb from the porchlight with a metal pair of needle-nosed pliers, pretty sure (but not definitely sure) that the power to the socket was shut off.

The other day on the phone he was telling me about how, after he'd finished installing a something-or-other for an elderly woman out in the country, he'd offered to cut her grass, just because. (A new sticker has appeared on his truck, "I am the warranty," which I love because it's always been true—word-of-mouth is the only advertising he's ever needed.) While cutting the woman's grass he grazed the electric fence for the cattle next door.

"I won't be doing that again."

I asked about the defibrillator installed in his chest, if he'd called the doctor's office to make sure the jolt hadn't shorted it out. He assured me it was fine: "They said, 'Oh, this happens a lot more often than you'd think.'"

Accidents will happen. I admire the way my wife's brother and his wife let their boys run and be boys, swinging sticks, throwing rocks, climbing walls and then jumping—they scrape a knee, they cry, they recover. Their parents make it look easy.

The last time I saw a baby fall down—this in a room full of children, with two sets of parent-friends—in that limbo moment where the child felt startled but hadn't yet decided to cry he saw the involuntary look of concern on my face and then decided, yes, I am going to burst into tears.

During our second ultrasound, the one at five months, the technician spent an hour searching out every part of the baby's little body, two raisin-sized kidneys, that elusive left ankle. Another image comes into focus. My wife cries and I laugh. Our baby has five toes on its right foot.

The baby is nestled into Anna's side with a little hand covering its little face, preventing the technician from getting a glimpse of the palate, and she warns us she may not be able to discern the baby's sex. The hour is nearly up before the baby shifts and the technician confirms her suspicion: It's a girl, it's definitely a girl. We are thrilled.

Then, driving home, we felt a baffling sadness. In regards to gender we hadn't had a strong preference either way, but we had settled, fairly firmly, on both a girl's name and a boy's name. Our boy was going to be Benjamin, Benjamin Anthony. He and I were going to share a middle name with my father and my grandfather and my father's grandfather. Now the boy we'd named and imagined was gone. Talking through it, Anna and I realized we were sad that we wouldn't come to know him.

People ask us the baby's name, but we're not telling, not yet. It's not a hard thing, except I want to tell my mother. I'll tell you: she's Hazel Elizabeth. Elizabeth is Anna's middle name, and Hazel was my mother's mother's first name. Hazel Elizabeth. Around the house we've been using it for weeks: "How's Hazel?" "Did we put it in Hazel's room?" "How's little Hazie Baby?"

Hazel my grandmother was a tiny woman when I knew her in her 80s, but she always seemed strong. She was the sexton of the Lutheran church I grew up in. She lived in the house beside the church, and she sat in the second pew from the

front every Sunday. She'd become,
my mother wrote recently,

> a widow when she was only in her for-
> ties. She was suddenly faced with rais-
> ing me (only in kindergarten) and my
> four siblings on her own. She relied
> on her faith to give her the strength to
> overcome her grief and provide for her
> children by working outside the home
> for the first time in her married life.

She grew up on a farm during the
Great Depression and saved the
plastic bag from every bread loaf
she ever bought. When she was a
girl she climbed trees. I wonder if
our girl will climb trees.

Who will she be? I wonder this
a lot—will she be shy or outgoing?
An artist or an athlete? What will
she love? These days I often dwell
in a pleasant sense of unknowing,
and I try not to let my imagination

pull me too far away from the reality of today.

I still need to anchor all our furniture to the walls, and Anna and I still haven't worked up the nerve to test our rental unit for lead paint—we worry a positive test might undo us. I've often worried that our house might be secretly trying to kill us, that the walls are harboring a terrible mold, that the cardboard boxes in the attic are ready to ignite, that the neighbors with whom we share a wall light thousands of candles each morning before they leave for work.

I mention the lead test to my parents, wanting reassurance, thinking Dad will put things in perspective. My mother says, "I'm sure I was exposed to lead paint when I was growing up and I turned out all right."

Sometimes comments like these are helpful, sometimes they aren't. A risk is a terrible thing that might happen, an image of a future that is possible but not certain. Like those ultrasounds of our baby, a risk is an image that can hold us rapt. It can demand our consideration, it can demand our obeisance—because a risk is also the image of a terrible thing that might *not* come to pass, a terrible thing that can maybe be avoided. Risk is never wrong. In that way it's a tyrant. Risk—if we let it—can become a terrible idol, an image that, even when accurate, pulls us away from the real.

My mother's nonchalance about the possibility of lead paint in the house surprised me. I've always assumed it was from my mother that I inherited my strong sense of caution. Where Dad habitually ignores the admonitions of doctors, Mom follows them to the letter and then some. If the doctor says don't lift more than fifteen pounds, she won't lift more than five, just to be safe. Whereas Dad, the day after an eye surgery, was out on the lawn tractor sucking up leaves in a large cloud of dust.

Halfway through the drive to drop me off at college, Dad would swap out *The Four Tops Live!* for *The O'Jays: Super Hits*, and then he'd toss an old sweatshirt over his face and fall asleep, leaving me to finish the drive, no worries at all about being chauffeured by someone so young. Mom was the opposite— tense the whole time, her hand hovering over an imaginary brake pedal on the dash. Absorbing her tension I became the erratic young driver she feared that I was.

My dad, if you haven't yet noticed, has always felt a little larger than life. (I once photoshopped him as a balloon peering out from behind a building in the Macy's Thanksgiving Day Parade, and he showed it to all the tellers at his bank.) Even now, when I go to the café in my hometown, I still sometimes get the age-old banter: "You're not Doug's kid, are you? I'm so sorry."

I smile. "Don't tell anybody."

At an icebreaker recently I was asked, "What fictional character do you most want to be like?" and "What fictional character are you *actually* most like?"

The first question, for me, was easy: Santiago from *The Old Man and the Sea*. It's his strength I admire, his physical and spiritual endurance, his conviction that "man is not made for defeat," that "a man can be destroyed but never defeated." (This, of course, is yet another way of saying I want to be like my dad.)

The second question was harder, requiring self-assessment and honesty. After much thought I figured it out. "Bilbo Baggins," I said, "but the way he is in the first chapter of *The Hobbit*."

Like both my parents I grew up in Central Pennsylvania, went to college in Central Pennsylvania, and I live and work in Central Pennsylvania—but like Bilbo I did eventually make my way to the mountains. When I learned I'd gotten into the MFA program at the University of Montana I was psyched and more than a little tipsy—my friend Jimmy and I, after the call came in over lunch, had ordered a second round based solely on the name of the beer: Victory Yakima Glory. That beer must have been about thirty percent ABV—we walked into my parents' house under what an old mentor of mine once called "the full sail of celebration." I was twenty-two years old.

Mom was at the kitchen sink. When I broke the news, her words came out before she could think: "Well you're not going." Those words, I know, came from love—

she didn't want me to move across the continent—but they hurt and I don't like writing them here. For a long time I held them against her, in a way that wasn't fair.

Anna loves feeling the baby move throughout the day, knowing when she's awake and when she's asleep. I'm reminded of Psalm 139: "You hem me in, behind and before," "You know when I sit and when I rise." I'm struck by how my daughter, for now, lives in a little universe that is benevolent entirely. She is almost literally surrounded by love.

"I wonder if we'll miss this," Anna says on our walk to church Sunday morning, "always knowing where she is, always knowing she's safe."

It's a thirty-six hour drive from my parents' house in Pennsylvania to the University of Montana if you do it in a car and stop only for gas. It took Dad and I two and a half days. We were in the cab of a U-Haul pulling my leaky Ford Explorer behind us. (That we made it over the Continental Divide still amazes me—Dad, I think, slept through those switchbacks.)

Several hours into North Dakota, we run out of 70s soul and classic rock, and we begin listening to recordings of my high school marching band performing songs by Chicago and Three Dog Night. We've been on the road for that long.

We'd slept in the cab the night before, after stopping late at a gas station in Wisconsin. A notice posted at the register said, "Beware of Feral Pigs." Tomorrow night we'll try to get a hotel room in Livingston, Montana, just north of Yellowstone, still three impossible hours east of Missoula and the University of Montana, but we'll be turned away from the first place we stop. No vacancy. It's Bike Week in Sturgis, South Dakota, and the place is full-up with a caravan of dazed-looking bikers.

But for now it's the flat green farmland of North Dakota, twenty-four hours of it (the world is so big!), with stops at every stray gas station so the truck doesn't give out—but then suddenly, at the far western side of the state, the farmland drops off and striped mountains come upon us out of nowhere, just beautiful, a place called Painted Canyon, our first glimpse of the West.

I look up the etymology of "adventure" to confirm a suspicion: it comes from an Old French word that means accident, but not only—it can refer also to a chance occurrence, an exciting incident, a remarkable event. A wonder, a miracle. "An account of marvelous things." As a verb it means to wander, to travel, to happen by chance. To risk loss, to reach, to arrive.

My father and I arrived in dust-dry Missoula on what for them was the most humid day of the summer. "It's usually not like this," the wilted shopkeepers kept telling us, but after roofing for months in the hot wet sponge that is Pennsylvania in summer, Dad and I unloaded the whole truck without breaking a sweat.

Weeks later a heavy package arrives in Missoula. It contains a can of diced tomatoes, a can of corn, a can of kidney beans, a can of black beans, two little cans of sliced olives, two packets of taco seasoning, a big bag of corn chips, an IOU for a pound of ground beef, browned and drained, and a note from my mother: "Combine and simmer for 1 hr. Top with crushed corn chips, shredded cheese, sliced black olives, sour cream, chopped green onion."

Here again I'm reminded of Psalm 139: "Where can I go from your Spirit? Where can I flee from your presence? If I go up to the heavens, you are there; if I make my bed in the depths, you are there. If I rise on the wings of the dawn, if I settle on the far side of the sea, even there your hand will guide me, your right hand will hold me fast."

My mother should have known I'd strike out for the mountains—she was the one who spent night after night reading to me aloud every chapter of *The Hobbit*. For my twelfth birthday she gave me a copy of *Around the World in Eighty Days*, a beautiful hardback covered in red velvet and gold letters, my favorite book for several years. I've put it on the shelf in the nursery along with several other books Hazel probably won't get to for a while: *A Wizard of Earthsea*, *A Wrinkle in Time*, *The Chronicles of Narnia*, *Catherine, Called Birdy*. (Is *True Grit* a novel appropriate for children?)

If my sense of caution comes from my mother, I'm coming to realize that I might owe her my adventurousness as well. She read aloud to me and my siblings every night— *The Boxcar Children*, *The Wizard of Oz*, *Watership Down*. (In *Watership Down* the intrepid rabbit who leads his fellow rabbits to safety is named Hazel.) As a little girl my mother spied on her sisters when their boyfriends came over. Like me she was a drummer in high school, and she too crossed the continent. Born the youngest of five in a small town in Pennsylvania, she took a Greyhound to California in the 80s, where she went to epic concerts. We tease her, saying she was there when Ozzy Osborne bit the head off a bat. She protests: "He was opening for Journey!"

She filled our house with piano music—with the Beatles and Vince Guaraldi and praise songs for church—and she never steered me or my siblings away from the drum set. I don't give her enough credit for shaping me into the person that I am. She's a psych major turned elementary school teacher, and we have long intense conversations about teaching.

Going through the baby's books I find a copy of *Peter Rabbit* my mother bought for the book-themed baby shower my sister put together. It was a decoration that stood by the vegetable tray, beside the *Green* [Deviled] *Eggs and Ham* sandwiches and the crockpot of *Cloudy-With-A-Chance-Of* meatballs, near the tray of *If-You-Give-A-Mouse-A* cookies.

I flip open the book and find an inscription from my mother:

Dear Granddaughter, We hope you have a life full of curiosity and adventures—just like Peter Rabbit!

Having no memory of the story I begin reading. Peter Rabbit's "adventure" begins with an admonition from his mother: "Don't go into Mr. McGregor's garden. Your Father had an accident there; he was put into a pie by Mrs. McGregor."

Put into a pie?

As a father-to-be I am horrified. This book, a facsimile of the first edition, contains an illustration (excised, I've learned, from later versions) of Mrs. McGregor serving a pie (presumably made of Peter's father) to Mr. McGregor, whose face is out of frame. He is two massive fists clenching a fork and a knife.

Mrs. Rabbit's warning, clearly, is a good one, but even if you've never read the book you know what comes next: "Peter, who was very naughty, ran straight away to Mr. McGregor's garden." I read on with trepidation—and that, I suppose, is the point. The folklorist Vladimir Propp has observed that in tales interdictions are always, inevitably, almost immediately disregarded—and of course they are. If protagonists don't violate interdictions they don't have any adventures worth telling.

But for a tale to take place you don't necessarily need an interdiction. "A command," writes Propp, "often plays the role of an interdiction. If children are urged to go out into the field or into the forest, the fulfillment of the command has the same consequences as does violation of an interdiction not to go into the forest or out into the field."

In other words, adventure is inevitable. No interdiction can ward it away, the garden awaits. We can only control our posture: Do we fear or do we send forth? I think for Anna and I it will always be both, but for now I'm struck by the way Mrs. Rabbit's interdiction is overturned by my mother's command: "Have a life full of curiosity and adventure." My mother's inscription, like a spell, transforms the text from a cautionary tale into a way of life, and I want to embrace it. There are certain experiences, risky ones from my childhood, that I hope my daughter will also get to have. For instance: I remember standing on a stool, my father's arms around me like roller coaster restraints—like the Lord in Psalm 139 his hands hold me fast—he's helping me guide a piece of wood through the band saw's whirring blade.

And so from an absurdly palatial Buy Buy Baby emporium I text him a picture, an image of little orange ear protectors, and I'm only half joking when I add the caption: "For when the baby learns how to use the drill press."

I write this last bit at the hospital— our six-pound baby was born early Sunday morning, after a labor that started slow and ended so fast the nurses and the doula were caught off guard by the baby's arrival. Mom and baby both are healthy.

There are many things I could tell you right now. I could tell you that Anna, whom I've always known to be a strong person, is stronger than I ever imagined. Or I could bring this essay full circle and tell you my father was right—I've never felt anything as soft as the bottoms of my baby's just-born feet. Or I could tell you that Anna is sleeping and I'm sitting here watching our son work through his first bout of hiccups.

Yes, our *son*. The birth happened so quickly that forty minutes went by before one of our nurses discovered that "Hazel" is a boy. She held him up, "Look at this." Our baby's left ankle was not the only body part to elude the ultrasound technician.

Accidents will happen and not all of them are bad. We're still wrapping our heads around this one—he was going to be Hazel Elizabeth. Now it looks like he might be Benjamin Anthony, that little boy we named and imagined and missed, and little Hazie is the child we won't (or won't yet?) get to know.

The nurses tell us this sort of mistake rarely happens anymore. They think the story is hilarious—forty minutes and no one noticed what should have been obvious. They keep dropping by our room to see our boy for themselves. "Is that—?" "Yes." Anna worries a little for the ultrasound tech—we suspect that, at least for a while, she's going to get relentlessly teased. The pediatrician is already making posters.

When I hold the baby I say to my son—(my son!)—I say, "Are you Benjamin? Are you Ben?" He looks at me with big eyes. We're neither of us sure just yet.

Acknowledgments

Thanks, first and foremost, to my friends and family, especially those of you who appear in these pages, named and unnamed. Especially Anna, and especially you, Ben. Thanks most of all to my mother and father, who have supported my writing since I was very small, not knowing how often they'd end up appearing in the work that I publish.

Thanks also to the writing teachers who have shown me the way and to my many former classmates at Susquehanna University and the University of Montana who helped me find my voice.

Thanks also to all the friends who have so generously read and responded to drafts of my work, both these pieces and others. I hesitate to start naming you, because I know I'll be leaving out so many, but I have to mention Louie and Megan Land, Casey Oliver, Bruce and Alison Van Patter, and, again, again, and again, Anna. (How many of my drafts have you read? Maybe a million—thank you.)

Thanks also to my students past and present. Talking about writing with you all, especially your own writing, is something that inspires me to keep going. And thanks to all my colleagues at Messiah University, who are the most wonderful people to work with.

Thanks also and again to Bruce Van Patter for his feedback on the design of this book, to Courtney Allen for her editorial services, to Megan Land for helping me cut through the red tape, and to the journals and presses that published earlier versions of these essays: Open Country Press, *The Common*, *The Good Men Project*, and *The Windhover*.

Last—and perhaps this should have been first—thanks be to God. I am grateful for everything.

Ryan Rickrode is the author of the novella *The Mountains May Depart*, published by Unsolicted Press. He received his MFA in fiction and creative nonfiction from the University of Montana in 2013 and has been writing and teaching in Central Pennsylvania ever since. As a senior lecturer in English at Messiah University, he teaches courses on creative writing, composition, and literature. His shorter work has appeared in various publications, including *Dappled Things*, *The Windhover*, and *The Cresset*. You can read more of his work at ryan-rickrode.com.

www.ingramcontent.com/pod-product-compliance
Lightning Source LLC
Chambersburg PA
CBHW051322120626
46547CB00015B/2358